I Say, I Say, I Say . . .

and other joke poems

8 21

Collected by John Foster

Illustrated by Chris Mould

OXFORD
UNIVERSITY PRESS

OXFORD
UNIVERSITY PRESS

Great Clarendon Street, Oxford OX2 6DP

Oxford University Press is a department of the University of Oxford.
It furthers the University's objective of excellence in research, scholarship,
and education by publishing worldwide in

Oxford New York

Auckland Bangkok Buenos Aires
Cape Town Chennai Dar es Salaam Delhi Hong Kong Istanbul
Karachi Kolkata Kuala Lumpur Madrid Melbourne Mexico City Mumbai
Nairobi São Paulo Shanghai Taipei Tokyo Toronto

Oxford is a registered trade mark of Oxford University Press
in the UK and in certain other countries

British Library Cataloguing in Publication Data available

ISBN 0-19-276312-1

1 3 5 7 9 10 8 6 4 2

Designed by Mike Brain Graphic Design Limited, Oxford

Printed in Great Britain by
Cox & Wyman Ltd, Reading, Berkshire

I Say, I Say, I Say . . .

Contents

I Say, I Say, I Say . . .

Ivan Jones

What is the difference
Between a big dark cloud
And a tiger with toothache?

One pours with rain
And the other roars
With pain!

Who is given the sack as soon as he starts work?
The coal man!

What did the big tap say to the little tap?
'You little drip.'
'Well,' said the little tap, 'if I'm a little drip
You must be a big leek.'

One day a dog saw a pigeon standing on one leg.
'Why are you standing on one leg?' it said.
'Because if I lifted the other
I'd fall over,' said the pigeon.

'Why does that horse look over that wall?' said the dog.
Because if he tried to look through it, he wouldn't be
able to see anything, of course.

Very Punny

Eric Finney

Dinah, on a video,
Saw a monster from long ago.
I'm not going to tell you any more:
Can you guess what monster Dinah saw?

A branch fell down and wrecked a truck.
Said the tree, 'I'm really sorry.
How are you feeling? What can I do?'
'Tremendous,' said the lorry.

The teacher asked for a sentence
That had the word **sycamore** in it.
'I'm sycamore homework,' said the girl
After thinking for a minute.

'Winter,' said the tree,
'Made my foliage disappear,
But I'm really relieved
Now that spring's here.'

Tick, Tock, Smash

Andrew Collett

My sister always drops her clock
from a window right up high,
to see for herself
if time can really fly!

The Bogeyman Cometh

Richard Caley

My brother swears a bogeyman
At night lurks by his head.
It serves him right, the dirty beast,
He picks his nose in bed.

What a Blow

Bill Condon

My nose was feeling ugly—
But I knew just the ticket,
I put it in a beauty contest . . .
The judges didn't pick it.

The Magician's Ghost

John Foster

The ghost of the magician said,
'I'm really in a fix.
The trouble is the audience
Sees right through all my tricks.'

Fowl Play

Clare Bevan

The roosters chanted,
'Ra! Ra! Ra!
The other team
We'll wreck 'em—
We're the kings
Of feathered things,
And we've got
David Peckem.'

They tackled hens,
They trampled wrens,
They pulverized an owl,
But when they cackled,
'We're the Champs!'
The other birds squawked,
'FOWL!!!!!'

The Day the Videoprinter Went Mad

Andrew Detheridge

I'll never forget the Saturday afternoon
the videoprinter went barking mad—

It began with what seemed a chance result:
    East Fife 5 Forfar 4
Then it followed it up with a plausible slip:
    Bolton 2 Pressed On 1
We really weren't too sure when we saw
    Southampton 3 Northampton 3
    Looton 1 Bognor 2
and we realized it had completely lost the plot
when it spewed out
    Motherwell 2 Mothercare 4
    West Ham 3 Boiled Ham 1
    Queen of the South 0 King of Spades 5

Suddenly, there was chaos in the studio,
voices could be heard panicking in the background—
but there was no stopping it:

    Chester 0 Drawers 0
    Crystal Palace 2 Buckingham Palace 1
    Leyton Orient 1 Orient Express 6
    Aston Vanilla 1 Birmingham Tutti Frutti 7

In desperation, they pulled the plug
and, slowly, the screen crackled
and fizzed like a dying firework.
But not before it had time
for a final parting finale:

> Ayr 1 Hydrogen 2
> Liverpool 0 Muddy Pool 2
> Wolves
>   0
>   Little
>   Pigs
>   3

And then it all went black.

The Art of Football

Tim Hopkins

Liverpool drew with Everton,
Arsenal and Tottenham coloured in.

Batty Books

John Foster

The Dead Parrot	by Polly Gone
Summer Holiday	by Sandy Beach
I've Got It!	by Penny Dropped
Christmas Decorations	by Holly and Ivy Bush
I Flew with the Dinosaurs	by Terry Dactyl
Rude Rhymes	by Ivor Cheek
How to Break a Window	by Eva Brickatit
Daydreamer	by Edna Cloud
Flashing Warnings	by Amber Light
A Life of Crime	by Robin Banks
Ocean Flier	by Albert Ross
I Can Make Your Mouth Water	by Candy Bar
Knick-Knacks and Dogs' Bones	by Paddy Wax
How to Be Gruff	by Billy Goat

Hot Dog

Trevor Harvey

'We're having a puppy for Christmas!'
My friend said, bright and perky;
And I replied, 'Oh, gosh—that's sad!
We always have a turkey.'

While Shepherds Watch

Richard Edwards

While shepherds watch their flocks by night
They sometimes fall asleep,
That's one of the big dangers when
Your job is counting sheep.

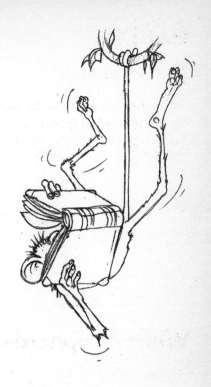

Good King Wenceslas

Richard Edwards

Good King Wenceslas looked out,
Snow was falling thickly,
'Got to get the shopping in,'
Said the king, 'and quickly.'
Jumped on to his mountain bike
Turned the pedals faster,
Skidded on a patch of ice,
Ended up in plaster.

Little Miss Fidget

Bill Condon

She fiddled with the stereo,
The washer, and the phone.
Anything with dials on
Was in her fiddle zone.
But now her hands are bandaged up,
She's resting for a while.
She did not read the sign that said:
'Don't touch the croc-o-dial.'

Seasick

Nick Toczek

'I don't feel whelk,' whaled the squid, sole-fully.
'What's up?' asked the doctopus.
'I've got sore mussels and a tunny-hake,' she told him.

'Lie down and I'll egg salmon you,' mermaid the
    doctopus.
'Rays your voice,' said the squid. 'I'm a bit hard of
    herring.'
'Sorry! I didn't do it on porpoise,' replied the doctopus
    orc-wardly.

He helped her to oyster self on to his couch
And asked her to look up so he could sea urchin.
He soon flounder plaice that hurt.

'This'll make it eel,' he said, whiting a prescription.
'So I won't need to see the sturgeon?' she asked.
'Oh, no,' he told her. 'In a couple of dace you'll feel
    brill.'

'Cod bless you,' she said.
'That'll be sick squid,' replied the doctopus.

One Word From Mary

Eric Finney

Mary Poppins, eating out,
Enjoyed her cauliflower cheese.
Followed that with two boiled eggs—
Which were bad and failed to please.
Mary crossly told the waiter
(And her tone was most ferocious!)
'Supercauliflowercheesebuteggswerequiteatrocious.'

All in a Name

John Foster

What do you call a girl with a calendar on her head?
June*
What do you call a girl with an oyster on her head?
Pearl
What do you call a boy with a car on his head?
Jack
What do you call a boy with a sports hall on his head?
Jim
What do you call a boy with a toilet on his head?
Lou
What do you call a boy with a speedometer on his head?
Miles
What do you call a girl with an elephant on her head?
Ellie
What do you call a girl with a sheep on her head?
Barbara

*Or May.

What's in a Roman Name?

Paul Cookson

Agrippa—well-known all-in wrestler
Hairgrippa—lesser known salon-owning brother

Jugula—Roman vampire
Regula—soldier of average size

Stickla—vicious slave-driver with no sense of humour
Tickla—not-so-vicious slave-driver with well-developed
    sense of humour

Claudius—emperor with long fingernails
Claudipus—emperor's cat

Agricola—farmer who invented fizzy soft drinks
Cherricola—his less-successful brother

Concordia—emperor with an aerodynamic nose
Baldus Cootius—emperor with aerodynamic head

A Right Shower!

Trevor Harvey

When the Romans landed in Britain,
The weather proved a teaser!
The emperor asked, 'Could this be *rain*?'
But the answer was, 'Hail, Caesar.'

Archimedes

Colin West

When Archimedes cried 'Eureka!'
And leapt out of his bath,
The people sighed, 'Another streaker!'
And kept out of his path.

Police Questioning

John Foster

Where does a police officer live?
999 Letsbe Avenue.

What do police officers eat in their sandwiches?
Truncheon meat.

Why are police officers good dancers?
They're always on the beat.

What do you call a police officer who shines a torch in
    your face?
A bobby dazzler.

What did the burglar say when he was arrested by a
    police officer with blonde hair?
It's a fair cop!

Lazy Brother

Andrew Collett

When I grow up I'm going to be a detective,
just like my older brother,
so I can spend all day in bed
working undercover!

Copped

Richard Edwards

The policeman was all bleary-eyed
From getting out of bed,
He fumbled with his razor
The shaving foam turned red—
He winced into the mirror,
'You're nicked,' the policeman said.

Nick (The Naughty Nicker*)

Bernard Young

When Nick went out nicking
he was caught
in the nick of time
and is now spending time
in the nick.

In his time
he's nicked knick-knacks,
a pickaxe,
a pick-up
a picture
and a picnic.

He's bad news.

If you need to choose
a new friend don't pick Nick.

(*He even nicked his nickname!)

A Pencil Case

John Rice

'So you say your school's been burgled.'
The policeman scratched his face.
'And there's nothing left to write with
—this looks like a pencil case.'

'Ello 'Ello 'Ello

Philip C. Gross

They burgled our nick the other day
Took handcuffs and truncheons and so on
They even took all the toilets away
The police say they've nothing to go on.

He Spied a Spider

Eric Finney

PC Plod became aware
Of a spider crawling his chest.
Attempting to catch the creature
He cried, 'Stop, you're under a vest!'

I Used to Climb Up Lamp-posts, Sir

Colin West

I used to climb up lamp-posts, sir,
At twelve o'clock at night.
I used to climb up lamp-posts, sir,
I knew it wasn't right.
I used to climb up lamp-posts, sir,
But now I've seen the light.

An Understanding Man

Colin West

I have an understanding
With an understanding man:
His umbrella I stand under
When I understand I can.

24

Unemployable

Gareth Owen

'I uth thu work in the thircuth,'
he said,
between the intermittent showers
that emerged from his mouth.
'Oh,' I said, 'what did you do?'
'I uth thu catth bulleth in my theeth.'

I'm Thor!

Anon.

The thunder god went for a ride
Upon his favourite filly.
'I'm Thor,' he cried.
And the horse replied,
'You forgot your thaddle, thilly!'

Have You Read . . . ?

Judith Nicholls

Enjoy your Homework	by R. U. Joking
Out for the Count	by I. C. Stars
Cliff-Top Rescue	by Justin Time
A Year in Space	by Esau Mars
Your Turn to Wash Up	by Y. Mee
Off to the Dentist	by U. First
Broken Windows	by E. Dunnett
Pickpocket Pete	by M. T. Purse
Lions on the Loose	by Luke Out
Helping Gran	by B. A. Dear
Ten Ice-creams	by Segovia Flaw
Rock Concert	by Q. Here

Tricky Quiz

Trevor Parsons

Can you surf on a microwave?
Can a saxophone be engaged?

How far can a front door step?
Why is a vacuum cleaner?

How long can a music stand?
How deep did the kitchen sink?

Which is louder—cold tap or hot?
How many rounds can a window box?

Just how far can a cricket pitch?
How fast can the sugar bowl?

Why is electric light?
Why is a cigarette lighter?

Dotty Definitions

John Foster

illegal: a bird of prey that is not very well
crowbar: a place where crows meet for a drink
bedlam: a cuddly sheep which sings a lullaby
category: a cat that has been in a fight
ramshackle: a sheep that has been tied up
bulldozer: a bull which is taking a nap
hobbyhorse: a horse that won't stop talking about stamp
  collecting
dormant: an ant which sleeps in a dormitory
dogma: what a dog's mother believes
toadstool: an implement used by a toad; also, a piece of
  furniture in a toad's house

Selection List for Knights of the Round Table

Brenda Williams

Sir Cumference Puts the enemy under siege,
Surrounds the castle with great ease.

Sir Tain Confident, positive, sure as fate.
Down to win, make no mistake.

Sir Render Always first to sense defeat,
Beat the drums, and cry retreat.

Sir Tificate Well qualified, his spurs hard won.
Takes the trophy when battle's done.

Sir Geon First on the battlefield after the fight,
Tends to the wounded, puts them
right.

Sir Vant He'll serve you well, for he is able
But serves you best around your table.

Sir Plus 'Let me fight,' this knight once pleaded
But though he's there, he's never
needed.

Sir Pent A snake in the grass you cannot trust.
He'll knife your back in one swift
thrust.

Sir Cumnavigate The flags of kings this knight's unfurled
While on his journeys round the world.

Sir Cus Travels around from town to town,
Amuses people, acts the clown.

Sir Viette Around your table he will linger,
You'll wrap him round your little finger.

Sir Cular Moats for castles, crowns for kings,
This knight keeps going round in rings.

The Dinosaurs That Time Forgot

David Harmer and Paul Cookson

The dinosaur whose feet hurt
. . . the Pawsaresorus

The singing dinosaur
. . . the Repeatachorus

The dinosaur who likes to be noticed
. . . the Don'tignorus

The dinosaur with a head like a mop
. . . the Wipethefloorus

The loyal dinosaur
. . . the Alwaysforus

The criminal dinosaur
. . . the Lawlessaurus

The one that lights up the sky
. . . the Auroraborealisaurus

The dinosaur that's just been to the dentist
. . . the Jawsaresorus

The dinosaur who lives in damp caves
. . . the Wallsareporus

The footballing dinosaur
. . . the Alwaysscorus

The DIY dinosaur
. . . the Hammernailandcopingsawus

The dinosaur that likes puzzles
. . . the Morejigsawus

The dinosaur found in a bedroom
. . . the Chestofdrawerus

The dinosaur built from coloured plastic bricks
. . . the Legosaurus

The toyshop dinosaur
. . . the ToysRusastaurus

A Small Dragon Verse

Paul Bright

It's not
The dragon in my plum tree
That disturbs me
I confess
But all day long
The plaintive cries
Of damsons in distress.

The Elephants' Dictionary

David Harmer

Elegant:	What elephants always are Especially at dinner.
Elevator:	How elephants go upstairs.
Elocution:	Polite trumpetings.
Elicopter:	Used by the elephant Flying Squad.
Elevision:	Home entertainment for the elephant (also known as ellytelly).
Elescope:	A long-sighted elephant.
Elepathic:	A far-sighted elephant.
Elephone:	For trunk calls.
Elementary:	Infants school for tiny tuskers.
Elegy:	Sad elephant's song.
Elements:	Rough weather for crossing the Alps.
Eletosis:	Bad breath on an elephant's tongue.
Elligator:	A snappy dresser among the pachyderms.

Central Eating

Anon.

Radi was a circus lion.
Radi was a woman hater.
Radi had a lady trainer.
Radiator.

Every Dog Has His Day

Nigel Gray

A crowded saloon in the old wild west:
A three-legged dog bursts through the door.
He goes to the bar and stares all round.
Says, 'I'm looking for the man who shot my paw.'

Thick Chick

Eric Finney

The chicken slept under a car
In spite of its mother's warning
And sure enough, before cock crow,
It woke oily the next morning.

Flea Transport

Eric Finney

Said the fly to the flea,
'You don't travel like me.
Do you progress by crawling or biking?'
Then the flea to the fly
Gave this crafty reply:
'I travel by itch-hiking.'

Bee Good

Eric Finney

Said baby bee to mother bee,
'No school today, I'll skive.'
Said mother bee to baby bee,
'No, you won't. Beehive.'

Signs of the Times

David Whitehead

Gone to the Loo
Back in a wee while!

Gone off in my time machine
Back last February.

Gone to see Doctor
Spooner—
Shan't lee bong—
Sack Boon

Gone to wind the town hall clock
Back in a tick

Gone to phone for an Ambulance
Back

Gone to Lynch
Signed Sheriff

Gone down the cellar
to find a gas leak
—Up in a flash!

Gone to Amnesia Therapy—
Back . . . er . . .

Gone to finish cutting
the lawn.
Back in half a Mo'

Popped to the paper shop to
buy a padded envelope.
Back in a Jiffy.

Attending a committee
meeting.
Back in a minute

Attending a course on self
Assertiveness—
I'll be back any time it
suits you.

True Love

Anon.

'Your teeth are like the stars,' he said,
And pressed her hand so white.
He spoke the truth, for, like the stars,
Her teeth came out at night.

Beauty Spots

Anon.

The rain makes all things beautiful,
The grass and flowers too.
If rain makes all things beautiful
Why doesn't it rain on you?

Fairground Attraction

Paul Cookson

I knew she was the one for me
The moment I saw her

My heart looped the loop
And helter-skeltered ever faster

But I was like the coconut.
Shy.

Dragon Love Poem

Roger Stevens

when you smile
the room lights up

and I have to call
the fire brigade

More Batty Books

John Foster

Flushed with Success	by Lou Chain
Eastern City Transport	by Rick Shaw
Strong Winds	by Gale Force
Watching Paint Dry	by Matt Finish
How to Cure Toothache	by Phil McCavity
Tummy Troubles	by Henrietta Jellyfish
Four Wheel Driving	by Alan Drover
Prize Draw	by Tom Bowler
How to Make Up	by Olive Branch
Christmas Tunes	by Carol Singer
Flotsam and Jetsam	by C. Shore
In the Nick of Time	by Arthur Second

Paws for Thought

Roger Stevens

My dog was staring at his feet,
Was it something he had caught?
Why no! My dog was thinking.
He was having paws for thought.

Bad Hare

Kaye Umansky

Harry Hare was late for school,
He dawdled in the lane.
He broke his brand new pencil
And his sums were wrong again.
He got sent off at football
And his homework blew away.
The teacher wrote his mum a note.
It was a Bad Hare Day.

Keep Your Hair, Ron!

Paul Cookson

Ron's wig cost a million pounds
I suppose that you could say
On Monday what he bought was
A high price toupee.

When Tuesday's whirlwind blew it off
All it brought was sorrow
For what he didn't know on Monday was . . .
Hair today gone tomorrow.

47

Blow-Dry Bill's a Baddie

Richard Caley

Blow-Dry Bill's a baddie
A hairdresser by trade
But at weekends he dons a mask
And does the odd bank raid.

He doesn't take a gun with him
No bullets does he fire,
Instead he takes a trusty friend
An old sawn-off hairdryer.

'How threatening can a hairdryer be?'
I hear you people say.
Well, if the staff don't give him cash
He blows them all away.

Cereal Disaster
(An Epitaph)

John Kitching

Here lies the body
Of Dickie Durrant.
Drowned eating muesli:
Pulled in by the currant!

Attack of the Mutant Mangoes— A Fruit Salad Ballad of Baddies

Andrew Fusek Peters

They are totally *bananas*
They hang out in a *bunch*
Don't *trifle* with these fruitcakes
Un-a-*peeling*, out to lunch.
They'll *orange* a nasty accident
And *prune* you down to size,
With hands around your *neck-tarine*
You'll end up in their pies.
They're evil, they're *extraberry*
And rotten to the core,
No more *pudding* up with them:
This is no food fight, it's a war!

Groan!

Richard Edwards

The baker's making bread,
His brow is hot and beaded,
The pummelled dough
Is happy though—
It's so nice to be kneaded.

The Butcher

Granville Lawson

In memory of Arnold Brown
A high class butcher of this town
Slipped while he was making mince
And nobody has seen him since
This may explain the reason why
I've really gone off shepherd's pie!

Cold Comfort

Nigel Gray

A party of Eskimos,
in their kayak at dawn,
lit a fire
to keep themselves warm.
The boat went down
with all its crew.
You can't have your kayak
and heat it too.

Speed

Granville Lawson

Jeffery won the hundred metres
At the annual High School sports.
Was it the diet and training that did it?
Or was it the wasp down his shorts?

End of Term Report

Granville Lawson

Dear Mr Bridle
Your son is bone idle.
I'm sorry to tell you he's thick.
Here's my report
On the poor little wart
It'll certainly make you feel sick:

GEOGRAPHY:	Thinks germs come from Germany.
SWIMMING:	Out of his depth.
ENGLISH:	Thinks a long sentence is ten years in prison.
FRENCH:	A failure.
MATHS:	Lazy. Thinks a cuboid is a boy from Cuba.
SCIENCE:	I have decided he has the brain of an earthworm.
MUSIC:	Doesn't know the difference between a trombone and a fishbone.
ART:	I wouldn't trust him to draw the curtains.
IT/COMPUTERS:	Oliver was excluded for feeding the mouse.
HISTORY:	Thinks Queen Victoria was named after a pub.

Index of Titles and First Lines

(First lines are in italics)

Acknowledgements

We are grateful for permission to reproduce the following poems:

Paul Bright: 'A Small Dragon Verse', from *Ha Ha! 100 Poems to Make You Laugh* (Macmillan 2001), copyright © Paul Bright, reprinted by permission of the author. **Paul Cookson:** 'Keep Your Hair Ron', from *Don't Get Your Knickers in a Twist* (Macmillan 2002), and 'What's in a Roman Name?', from *Roman Poems* (Macmillan), copyright © Paul Cookson 2002, reprinted by permission of the author. **Paul Cookson and David Harmer:** 'The Dinosaurs That Time Forgot', from *Spill the Beans* (Macmillan), copyright © Paul Cookson and David Harmer, reprinted by permission of the authors. **Bill Condon:** 'What a Blow', and 'Little Miss Fidget', from *Don't Throw Rocks at Chicken Pox* (Angus & Robertson), copyright © Bill Condon 1993, reprinted by permission of the author. **Richard Edwards:** 'Good King Wenceslas', and 'While Shepherds Watch', from *Nonsense Christmas Rhymes* (Oxford University Press 2002), 'Copped', from *Teaching the Parrot* (Faber 1996), 'Groan!', from *The House that Caught a Cold* (Viking 1991), copyright © Richard Edwards, all reprinted by permission of the author. **David Harmer:** 'The Elephant's Dictionary', from *Elephant Dreams* (Macmillan), copyright © David Harmer, reprinted by permission of the author. **Gareth Owen:** 'Unemployable', from *Salford Road*, copyright © Gareth Owen 1976, reprinted by permission of the author. **John Rice:** 'A Pencil Case', from *School's Out* (Oxford University Press), copyright © John Rice, reprinted by permission of the author. **Nick Toczek:** 'Seasick', from *Ha Ha! 100 Poems to Make You Laugh* (Macmillan 2002), copyright © Nick Toczek, reprinted by permission of the author. **Kaye Umansky:** 'Bad Hare', from *Nonsense Animal Rhymes* (Oxford University Press), copyright © Kaye Umansky, reprinted by permission of the author. **Colin West:** 'I Used to Climb Up Lamp-posts, Sir', and 'Archimedes', from *Not to be Taken Seriously* (Hutchinson), copyright © Colin West 1982, and 'An Understanding Man', from *It's Funny When You Look At It* (Hutchinson) copyright © Colin West 1984, all reprinted by permission of the author.

All other poems are published for the first time in this collection by permission of their authors.

Clare Bevan: 'Fowl Play', copyright © Clare Bevan 2003 **Richard Caley:** 'The Bogeyman Cometh' and 'Blow-Dry Bill's a Baddie', copyright © Richard Caley 2003 **Andrew Collett:** 'Tick Tock Smash', and 'Lazy Brother', copyright © Andrew Collett 2003 **Paul Cookson:** 'Fairground Attraction', copyright © Paul Cookson 2003 **Andrew Detheridge:** 'The Day the Videoprinter Went Mad', copyright © Andrew Detheridge 2003 **Eric Finney:** 'Very Punny', 'One Word From Mary', 'He Spied a Spider', 'Thick Chick', 'Flea Transport', and 'Bee Good', copyright © Eric Finney 2003 **John Foster:** 'The Magician's Ghost', 'All in a Name', 'Police Questioning', 'Dotty Definitions', 'Batty Books', and 'More Batty Books', copyright © John Foster 2003 **Nigel Gray:** 'Every Dog Has His Day', and 'Cold Comfort', copyright © Nigel Gray 2003 **Philip C. Gross:** ''Ello, 'Ello, 'Ello', copyright © Philip C. Gross 2003 **Trevor Harvey:** 'Hot Dog' and 'A Right Shower!', copyright © Trevor Harvey 2003 **Tim Hopkins:** 'The Art of Football', copyright © Tim Hopkins 2003 **Ivan Jones:** 'I Say, I Say, I Say', copyright © Ivan Jones 2003 **John Kitching:** 'Cereal Disaster', copyright © John Kitching 2003 **Granville Lawson:** 'The Butcher', 'Speed', and 'End of Term Report', copyright © Granville Lawson 2003 **Judith Nicholls:** 'Have You Read...?' copyright © Judith Nicholls 2003 **Trevor Parsons:** 'Tricky Quiz', copyright © Trevor Parsons 2003 **Andrew Fusek Peters:** 'Attack of the Mutant Mangoes', copyright © Andrew Fusek Peters 2003 **Roger Stevens:** 'Dragon Love Poem', and 'Paws for Thought', copyright © Roger Stevens 2003 **David Whitehead:** 'Signs of the Times', copyright © David Whitehead 2003 **Brenda Williams:** 'Selection List for Knights of the Round Table', copyright © Brenda Williams 2003 **Bernard Young:** 'Nick (The Naughty Nicker)', copyright © Bernard Young 2003